# The Spacesuit

## How a seamstress helped put man on the moon

Written by
**Alison Donald**

Illustrated by
**Ariel Landy**

**October 1963**
Cosmonaut Valentina Tereshkova
becomes the first woman in space.

**December 1968**
Apollo 8 first to go around the
moon with people inside.

**July 16 1969**
Apollo 11 blasts off

**July 20 1969**
Man walks on
the moon

This is Ellie.

Ellie helped change the world with a needle and thread many years ago.

The [...] book...

Thi[...] e" Foraker.
Elean[...] worked at
ILC Dove[...] s and manager,
Ellie [...] f spacesuits.
She also [...] d inflatable oil
[...] issions.

In memory of Eleanor Foraker
(2nd Sept 1930 – 3rd Dec 2011)
and dedicated to the women and men
who worked tirelessly behind the
scenes to make the moon landings
possible. Thank you.

Ellie

*The Spacesuit*
An original concept by author Alison Donald
© Alison Donald
Illustrated by Ariel Landy

MAVERICK ARTS PUBLISHING LTD
Studio 3A, City Business Centre, 6 Brighton Road, Horsham
West Sussex, RH13 5BB, +44 (0)1403 256941
© Maverick Arts Publishing Limited

Published June 2019

A CIP catalogue record for this book
is available at the British Library.

**ISBN 978-1-84886-428-3**

Maverick
publishing
www.maverickbooks.co.uk

distributed in US by
Lerner

*October 1957*
The first satellite is launched
into space by Russia.

*May 1961*
John F. Kennedy challenges America
to put a man on the moon.

*April 1961*
Cosmonaut Yuri Gagarin
becomes the first man in space.

*February 1962*
Astronaut John Glenn goes around
the earth in a spacecraft.

Ellie loved to design and sew from a young age.

As a child, she felt her fingers come alive
the first time she used a sewing machine.
She threaded the needle and pressed the foot pedal.

The sewing machine launched
her into another universe.

Where fabric could be tucked and tapered. The whir of the machine fuelled her imagination with ideas. With hard work, any design was possible.

As an adult, Ellie got a job sewing clothing for women and babies.

Ellie worked quickly and carefully. Her seams were straight and her stitching was neat. An engineer noticed and asked her a question.

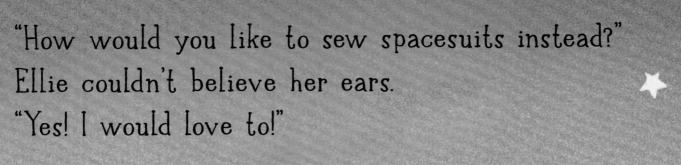

"How would you like to sew spacesuits instead?"
Ellie couldn't believe her ears.
"Yes! I would love to!"

If we win, our spacesuit will go to the moon!

FACT:
Ellie worked for a company called ILC Dover. Their division, Playtex, made bras and cloth nappies!

Ellie's workplace had entered an exciting competition at the last minute.

But it wasn't going to be easy.

SPACESU
COMPETI

Does your com
have what it take

FACT: It wasn't unusual for the undergarment industry to try new things. In World War One they designed flight suits for pilots.

Big teams of military designers and engineers were also competing.
Ellie's team was small, and they only had six weeks.
Many believed that seamstresses could never win.

But Ellie ignored them and set to work.

Thankfully Ellie had help.

She worked with Lenny and his team of engineers.
Some engineers were so impressed with the women's sewing that
they asked if the seamstresses could teach them how to sew.

The seamstresses also shared ideas about how to best make the suit. Ellie looked up old spacesuits.

"They're hard like armour."

"Can we make something softer and more comfortable?"

The answer was yes.

The plan was to make a spacesuit with many soft layers.

The seamstresses worked from dawn until dusk.

The stitching was slow and if they made a mistake, the whole suit was thrown out.

As the suits got bulkier the seamstresses complained.

FACT:
The suits got so bulky that the seamstresses had trouble feeding them through their sewing machines.

Two gigantic sewing machines appeared.
The ladies named them: 'Sweet Sue' and 'Big Moe'.

FACT:
The seamstresses had to sew within 1/64 of an inch! That is the width of a pin!

Ellie stitched late into the night with
Lenny helping by her side.

As the competition drew near the women were exhausted.
But everyone pulled together.
The women sewed and glued layer after layer until...

...they had 21 layers!

Finally the A7L spacesuit was created.

The suits were tested and rushed off to Texas for judging when...

FACT:
The seamstresses were so proud of the spacesuit that some of them signed their names on the inside.

...the judges noticed a broken zipper.

Ellie and her team were given 12 hours to fix it and return it to the judges.

The suit made it just in time
(with help from an airplane!).

After many tests, the results were in.

The first competitors'
suit failed because
the helmet blew off!

**FACT:**
The spacesuits were tested in special areas that had reduced gravity – just like the moon!

The second competitors' suit failed because it was too wide to fit in the space capsule.

Lastly the A7L spacesuit...

On 20<sup>th</sup> July 1969 when Neil Armstrong and Buzz Aldrin walked on the moon, Ellie and her team were nervous.

But when she saw them pick up moon rocks and return to the capsule safely, Ellie knew the suits were perfect.

Ellie's heart
swelled with pride.

The universe seemed smaller that night.

The earth and the moon felt woven together
by invisible thread.

Stitch by stitch, layer by layer, the A7L
spacesuit had changed the world forever.

# Glossary

### Apollo 11
The name of the spaceflight that landed on the moon. This was manned by Neil Armstrong, Edwin "Buzz" Aldrin and Michael Collins.

### Astronaut / Cosmonaut
A person who goes into space. A cosmonaut is the name for an astronaut of the Soviet or Russian space programme.

### Engineer
Someone who designs and makes things.

### Latex
Latex makes clothing soft and fitted.

### JLC Dover / Playtex
This is the company that made the A7L. They are based in Delaware, USA. Ellie worked for Playtex, which was best known for making undergarments (bras, nappy covers, girdles)!

### Seamstress
A woman who sews for her job. Today, women or men who sew for their jobs can be called a 'sewer' or 'garment maker'.

My team and our spacesuit!

Scan the QR code to find out more!